THE BIGGEST GIRL IN THE WORLD

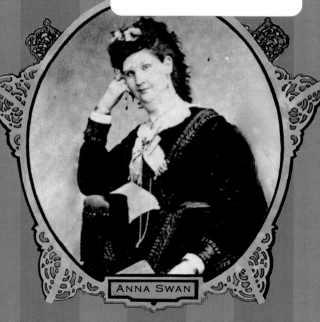

ANNA SWAN

BY JOANNE STANBRIDGE
ILLUSTRATED BY DRAZEN KOZJAN

THE BIGGEST GIRL IN THE WORLD

STANDING TALL

"Stand up tall," said Anna's grandmother. "Be proud of who you are!" Anna tried, but it wasn't easy. She had to duck through doorways and stoop low to shake hands. People stared. Some were even afraid of her. She was the biggest person they had ever seen.

QUESTION GENERATE

What questions could you ask?

All her life, Anna Haining Swan had been different from other children. On the day she was born, she was already as big as a six-month-old child. By her fourth birthday, she was tall enough to wear her mother's dresses. And still she kept growing. It might have been easier if her parents and her six brothers and sisters had been big, too, but they were all average-sized. Only Anna was big.

These days, doctors know that her unusual size was caused by the pituitary gland in her brain. But in 1846, the year Anna was born in Nova Scotia, Canada, doctors hadn't discovered this condition and couldn't treat it. So she grew and grew and grew.

WORD ORIGIN pituitary Where's it from?

SETTING ANALYSIS

How do you think the setting of 1846 will affect Anna's life?

As a teenager, Anna longed to be like other girls, but her size kept setting her apart. At home, her father had to knock down a wall to make room for her extra-large bed. She couldn't fit into normal chairs. At school, she had to sit on a tall stool at a desk propped up higher by planks. At mealtimes, she sat on the floor, holding the tiny teacups between two fingers. One day, she sat on the end of a bench. The bench tipped up like a see-saw, and the woman on the other end went flying!

CHARACTER ANALYSIS

What kind of person do you think Anna was? Why?

Anna spent hours by herself, reading and dreaming. She loved books. She wished she could be a teacher – but it hurt even to dream about that. A few weeks studying at a teacher's college in another town only made her miserable. She had to squeeze herself into a little desk and struggled to sleep in a normal-sized bed. She tried to ignore the rude stares of the other students and even some of the teachers. She pretended not to see the strangers who drove around town, hoping to get a glimpse of her. It was no use. Homesick and tormented by strangers, Anna soon gave up. She went home.

She didn't know that her life would soon be wilder than her wildest dreams. She had no idea that she would soon be rich, famous, in danger . . . and in love.

PREDICT

What do you think could happen in Anna's life?

THE GIANT GIRL

One day, a mysterious visitor arrived from New York City. He'd heard a lot of rumours. Were they true? Was "the giant girl" really as big as people said? He climbed onto a chair to measure Anna's height. He wrote down her weight. A tape measure that passed once around her waist went twice around his own. At fifteen years of age, Anna was 241 centimetres tall (7 feet 11 inches) and she weighed 182 kilograms (more than 400 pounds).

The stranger was thrilled. Anna was the biggest woman he had ever seen – and that was saying something, because this man had shaken hands with plenty of unusual people. He had worked with the shortest man in the world, who could walk under a table without ducking, and the skinniest, who was called "the Living Skeleton". Now he wanted to work with Anna. He made an offer.

OPINION Do you think a museum like Mr Barnum's would be acceptable in today's society? Why or why not?

The mysterious stranger was an agent for the famous showman P.T. Barnum. In those days, everyone knew about Mr Barnum's American Museum in New York City. It was crowded with wonders: real live whales, Siamese twins, fortune-tellers, fun-house mirrors, exotic shoes, a new-fangled sewing machine, a trained seal named Ned and many other wonders.

Now Mr Barnum's agent made Anna an offer. If she would move to New York and be a "living exhibit" in the American Museum, he would give her a good salary, beautiful clothes and a chance to be famous. To sweeten the deal, he offered her a new carriage. It would be extra-large, built specially for Anna. With a carriage like that, she could ride through the streets of New York in comfort and style.

Anna's family didn't have much money, and in those days few careers were open to women. Even fewer were open to giants. This was the chance of a lifetime. Still, Anna was uncertain. She loved books, she loved to learn and she longed to be a teacher.

"Mr Barnum can help with that, too," the agent promised. "Come to New York and see for yourself."

SETTING
PREDICTION

How do you think the setting of New York will be different? Do you think it will affect Anna? How?

A Dream Come True

In 1862, Anna and her parents went to New York City to meet Mr Barnum and see his museum. They couldn't believe their eyes. The building was plastered with posters advertising the bizarre exhibits. On a balcony over the street, a band played loud music. Mr Barnum paid the musicians to play badly so people would hurry into his museum to get away from the noise!

New York City was a long way from the village on Canada's east coast where Anna grew up. She and her parents were tired from their journey. Even so, she was excited and nervous as she stepped from the carriage. Remembering her grandmother's advice, she stood up tall and proud. In the street, people stopped and stared, but Anna held her head high.

She and her parents went into the museum to meet the famous showman. Mr Barnum liked Anna right away. She was seventeen years old, well-spoken and graceful. Later, he said of her, "She was an intelligent and by no means ill-looking girl." He was ready to sign her up on the spot, but Anna refused to rush. She took her time and studied the contract carefully.

If she signed it, Mr Barnum would expect her to be on display in the museum every day for three years. In return, he would give her everything his agent had offered, plus three hours of lessons each day with a private tutor and plenty of money to buy books. The tutor would also act as a chaperone and companion while Anna was in New York.

Even in her happiest dreams, Anna had never imagined having her own private teacher. She signed the contract.

QUESTION GENERATE
What questions could you ask?

chaperone

CLARIFY

THE MUSEUM FAMILY

At first, Anna's new job as "the Tallest Woman in the World" was painful and difficult. She had to stand in the museum while people stared and stared at her. They couldn't see who she really was. They couldn't see into her heart or her mind, and they didn't know how clever and kind she was. They only knew that she was very, very big.

All her life, Anna had been struggling to blend in with average-sized people. Now she was expected to stand up straight and look as tall as possible. When she piled her hair on top of her head to gain a bit more height, she reached a height of 246 centimetres (8 feet 1 inch). She wore a gorgeous gown, specially made for her at a cost of more than $1000, that made her look more imposing than ever.

QUESTION

How do you know Anna was not happy about how she looked?

Why was the museum setting important for Anna's new job? What might her job have been like in a different setting?

As a finishing touch, she stood next to one of the smallest people in the world. His name was Commodore Nutt, and he was just 73 centimetres (2 feet 5 inches) tall. The top of his head barely reached Anna's knees. If she was careful, she could pick him up in one hand.

Next to Anna, Commodore Nutt looked smaller than ever. Next to him, she looked truly gigantic. Thousands of people flocked to see them. Mr Barnum was delighted.

WORD ORIGIN

auditorium   Where's it from?

QUESTION

Why do you think Anna
was accepted in the
museum family?

Some of the people who came to see the "Lady Giant" were respectful. Others whispered, giggled and made jokes. At first Anna didn't know what to do, but slowly she learned to ignore them, even when she was angry and upset. It wasn't easy.

Her colleagues at the museum helped. They knew how Anna felt. Little Commodore Nutt and the thin man called the Living Skeleton soon became her friends.

So did Lavinia Warren, an intelligent woman who was even smaller than Commodore Nutt. Lavinia had been a teacher before she was hired to work at the museum, and she loved books almost as much as Anna did. Before long, Anna became part of this "museum family".

Mr Barnum discovered that Anna was a good thinker and an excellent speaker. He invited her to give some lectures in the third-floor auditorium. Anna felt right at home on the stage, teaching audiences about the medical condition that causes people to become giants.

CHARACTER ANALYSIS

Why do you think so many people came to see Anna? What can you infer about her character?

DISASTER!

One day, when Anna was giving a lecture, smoke began to swirl through the hall. The museum was on fire!

In those days, there were no automatic fire alarms or sprinklers. The wooden floors and walls were the perfect food for the fire, which raced through the museum like a wild animal. Flames gobbled up the ground floor, spreading so fast that people had to run for the doors. Wax statues of Napoleon and Queen Victoria burst into flames. The fortune-teller and the one-armed weight-guesser crowded towards the exit with their frightened customers. Upstairs, the smell of smoke and sounds of confusion interrupted Anna's talk.

By the time Anna's audience realised what was happening, the fire was roaring up the stairs. People jumped to their feet and rushed to escape. Some of them began to scream.

Anna hurried towards the main staircase, but thick smoke knocked her back. She ran for the back stairs, but they were narrow and flimsy. The fire had weakened them. She couldn't get out!

SETTING
ANALYSIS
The setting has changed in some way.
What words would describe it now?

QUESTION

What words might describe
the feelings of Anna and
the people now?

15

Outside, horse-drawn fire engines rumbled through the streets with their bells clanging. A huge crowd choked the road. Smoke boiled from the windows and doors of the museum.

Anna struggled to a window, but it was too high for even the tallest fire ladder to reach her. But, in a street nearby, construction workers had been using a crane. Rescuers dragged it towards the burning building and climbed upwards. Swinging picks and sledgehammers, they smashed the wall around the window until the opening was big enough for Anna to squeeze through.

CHARACTER PREDICTION

Thinking about Anna's character, predict what you think she might do now.

Someone knotted together a makeshift harness with ropes and pulleys. Terrified, Anna put it on and inched across the window ledge then swung out into thin air. Eighteen men held tight to the lines as she dangled high over the street. If they let go, or if she slipped, she would tumble to her death.

At last, the rescuers lowered Anna safely to the ground and a great cheer went up from the crowd. Someone helped her into a carriage and, as she rode away to safety, Anna realised that she had barely escaped with her life. Only a few minutes ago, she had been giving a lecture, and now the museum was gone, and with it her life as she knew it.

A FRESH START

Mr Barnum's museum was completely destroyed by the fire. Luckily, none of Anna's friends was hurt, but all of her belongings were gone: her books and letters, her beautiful clothes and her entire life savings of $1200. To Anna, it may have seemed like the end of the world. But it wasn't.

Before the fire, Mr Barnum had already taken Anna on a tour to Europe where she had been a sensation. She had been presented to Queen Victoria of England, who was charmed by her dignity and grace. Now another European tour followed. By the time she returned home, Anna had become world famous.

In 1871, she was about to make her third trip to Europe when she discovered that the group of entertainers touring with her included someone she found very interesting. Martin Van Buren Bates had fought on the Southern side in the American Civil War and reached the rank of captain. He was also very handsome, and at 241 centimetres (7 feet 9 inches) he was almost as tall as she was.

Anna and Martin soon found they had a great deal in common and, before the end of the week-long sea voyage to England, the couple had announced their engagement.

QUESTION

What is meant by:

. . . charmed by her dignity and grace . . . ?

OPINION Do you think Anna should have continued to work for Mr Barnum? Why or why not?

INFERENCE

What can you infer about the type of life Martin might have had?

19

QUESTION

Why do you think people's attitudes towards Anna have changed from the beginning of the book?

It was an exciting time for Anna and Martin. Everybody wanted to see the giant couple, and their public appearances were an enormous success. Anna made her second visit to Queen Victoria, this time accompanied by her husband-to-be, and they were each presented with a gold watch. The Queen also gave Anna a diamond ring and a beautiful wedding dress.

At their wedding in a church in London's Trafalgar Square, the streets were crowded with people hoping to catch a glimpse of the extraordinary pair in their wedding finery. Later, Martin and Anna left for their honeymoon in a **carriage decorated** with **dangling boots by the neighbours of their new London house.**

Back in London, and busy with royal receptions and tour arrangements, Anna learned that she was to have a baby. In May 1872, she gave birth to a girl who was as big as she had been when she was born – 8 kilograms (18 pounds). But, though the most famous doctors of the time were there to attend her, the baby died. Broken-hearted, Anna and Martin returned to the United States and bought a large plot of land in Seville, Ohio.

WORD ORIGIN honeymoon Where's it from?

INFERENCE

What can you infer from:

Anna and Martin returned to the United States and bought a large plot of land . . . ?

21

Life In Ohio

Anna was still young and there was always hope of another baby. Meanwhile, Anna and Martin set about building a future to match their giant-sized requirements. Their new home's ceilings would be 4.2 metres (14 feet) high, and the doorways 2.6 metres (8.5 feet) high – built extra wide for comfort.

The furniture they had made for the sitting room was so big, the ladies at their house-warming party refused to sit down. They felt it wasn't dignified to climb or be lifted onto a sofa or chair. Martin and Anna couldn't help feeling a little amused to see their guests struggling to fit in, just as they always had.

Many of their "museum family" came to stay, including the Living Skeleton, the Siamese twins and Lavinia.

Anna and Martin had some unusual pets, including a monkey named Buttons and a boa constrictor.

QUESTION

What do you think is meant by:
. . . struggling to fit in . . . ?

22

QUESTION
GENERATE
What questions could
you ask?

SETTING
ANALYSIS

How do you think this new setting will
affect Anna and Martin's life?

CLARIFY   deteriorated

Martin had a special carriage built and the couple paid visits in the community, making many new friends, especially among the local children. Martin would wear his uniform around the town, hoping for a reaction. And Anna was at last able to live out a little of her childhood teaching dream by taking Sunday School classes.

They also began touring again, this time with the W.W. Cole Circus. They travelled with the circus to dozens of mining towns in the western United States.

Then, in 1878, Anna discovered she was pregnant again. It was a difficult birth. At nearly 10 kilograms (22 pounds), their new baby son was even bigger than their first child and, tragically, he lived for just eleven hours. Devastated, Martin and Anna tried to distract themselves by touring with the circus, but Anna's health had begun to deteriorate and they decided to retire for good.

SETTING
ANALYSIS

What influence do you think the setting of the 1870s had on Anna and her babies?

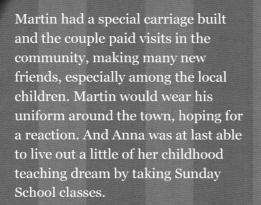

QUESTION

Why do you think Anna and Martin went back to performing in the circus?

In 1882, old friends at a circus gathering were struck by Anna's pale, thin face. She rested more and more often and even gave up teaching Sunday School. Then, just before her forty-second birthday, she died. Crowds gathered for her funeral and to see her buried beside her baby son.

Anna Swan Bates did not live a long life, but it was an extraordinary, often exciting one. She sailed the ocean, toured Europe and chatted with the Queen of England. And she found happiness with her husband and friends in a much-loved home. Instead of squeezing herself into a too-small world, Anna grew up to live a life that fitted her perfectly well . . . with plenty of room to grow.

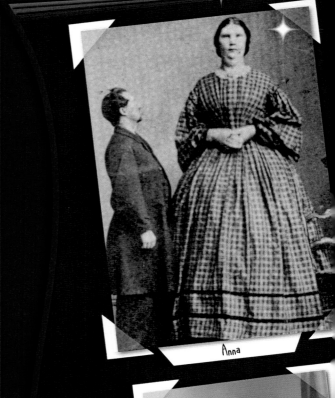

Anna

TIMELINE
OF THE MAIN EVENTS IN ANNA'S LIFE

Birth	?	?	?	?	?
1846	?	?	?	?	?

P.T. Barnum

Wedding day

Anna and Martin with average-sized people

Museum family: Tom Thumb, Lavinia Warren, Commodore Nutt, Minnie Warren

THINK ABOUT THE TEXT

What connections can you make to the emotions, situations or characters in The Biggest Girl in the World?

being different

facing prejudice

gaining self-confidence

Text to Self

overcoming obstacles

finding friends

being successful

inspiring people

TEXT TO TEXT

Talk about other stories you
may have read that have similar
features. Compare the stories.

TEXT TO WORLD

Talk about situations in the world
that might connect to elements in
the story.

PLANNING A BIOGRAPHY

1 Choose a person that you want to write about. Write some questions you have about the person.

- When was she born?
- What was she well known for?
- What was her childhood like?
- What education did she have?
- What were her achievements?
- What were her disappointments?
- Did she have any children?
- When did she die?

2 Interview the person or resear them at the library or on the Internet. Make notes.

Anna Swan:
- Born in Nova Scotia in 18
- Famous for being bigger th other people.

3 Look at your notes and make a plan. Can you use timelines, sketches, photographs?

birth/death

personal life

childhood

Anna Swan

character

education

disappointments

achievements

4 Use your plan to write the biography.

Writing a Biography

Have you . . .

- written in the third person?

- recorded events in order of time?

- highlighted the significant events in the person's life?

- included details about their childhood, education, character, career achievements, disappointments and personal life?

- avoided author opinion or bias?

- included quotes from people who knew the person?

- included photographs and timelines?

Don't forget to revisit your writing. Do you need to change, add or delete anything to improve your writing?